Different, Not Dumb

A Young Girl's Journey with Dyslexia

J. Postell

Different, Not Dumb

Designed by 5.13 Graphics & Media, LLC and AI

ISBN 979-8-9920972-6-9

Printed in USA
https://www.thejuniorauthors.com/different-not-dumb.html#/

DEDICATION

This book is dedicated to every child who learns differently. May your unique way of learning help others see the world in color. The world needs the brilliance that only you can bring.

DIFFERENT WAYS WE LEARN (VARK)

Did you know that people learn in different ways?

VISUAL LEARNERS

Visual learners understand information best when they can see it. They learn well through pictures, videos, charts, diagrams, and illustrations.

AUDITORY LEARNERS

Auditory learners learn best by listening. They enjoy lectures, discussions, music, audiobooks, podcasts, and hearing information explained out loud.

KINESTHETIC LEARNERS

Kinesthetic learners learn best by doing. They enjoy hands-on activities, experiments, building things, and moving around while they learn.

READING/WRITING LEARNERS

Reading/Writing learners understand information best through words. They like reading books, writing notes, making lists, and explaining ideas through writing.

Everyone's brain learns differently—and that's a good thing!

WHICH LEARNER ARE YOU?

Different, Not Dumb
A Young Girl's Journey with Dyslexia

DUMB is such a mean word. It's an insult, a label, a bad word placed on people who learn differently. For a long time, I thought that word described me.

There were times when the entire class seemed to understand things I didn't. Everyone had the answers while I was still trying to understand the question. Why was school so hard for me?

It must be because I'm the dumb one!

My mother said she always did well in school. She got good grades and loved all of her classes. Maybe that's where my sister got it from. She did well in school just like mom. I often imagined her in class raising her hand because she had all the answers.

Why didn't I ever have the answers? Why did listening to the teacher explain certain math problems make my head spin?

It must be because I'm the dumb one!

I hated it when the teacher called on me, and I didn't know the answer. She would stand there waiting, expecting me to say something. It felt like the whole room was watching, and the silence lasted forever.

Why didn't I learn as quickly as everyone else? I had more questions than answers, and the harder I tried to understand, the more confused I became.

My sister was the valedictorian of her high school class. I was so proud of her. Unfortunately, I wasn't smart enough to be valedictorian.

She was even in a special magazine for smart children. Everybody saw it. Why wasn't I smart enough to get into a fancy magazine?

It must be because I'm the dumb one!

SUPERSTAR SISTER!

Our church rewarded students who made the honor roll with money. Ten dollars for every A. Five dollars for every B. I never made the honor roll. I never got any money.

When was my brain going to start acting right? I wanted to make my mother proud by walking to the front of the church and receiving money for good grades, but that never happened.

I didn't like school because I never felt seen, heard, or understood. I enjoyed learning. I really did. Certain subjects made sense to me, while others went right over my head like an airplane.

I thought I would be the dumb one, forever.

I would never make the honor roll.

Never be in a magazine.

Never be at the head of my class.

Never get money for good grades.

Never be anything but the dumb one!

NEVER...
NEVER...
NEVER...

Most of the time, I was just bored.
My teacher would say, "Add the 2 and carry the 1."
I hated carrying the 1, and I especially hated rounding numbers.

Math was my arch nemesis. My kryptonite. The evil villain to my superhero. My mother said math could be fun, but she was wrong. Math was never fun!

22 + 78 + 14

CARRY THE 1

I wanted learning to be colorful like my crayons.
Creative like my art teacher.
Fun like my gym teacher.
I wanted knowledge to dance in my head like my favorite song.
I wanted learning to be entertaining like my favorite movie, and silly like my friends, but it wasn't like any of that.

7+5=
12-4=?

Reading wasn't so bad. I actually enjoyed reading.

I especially enjoyed spelling tests. I could spell some pretty large words.

Permitted.

P-E-R-M-I-T-T-E-D…

I am permitted to leave if I don't enjoy this class!

Permitted.

P-E-R-MITTED
Permitted.

Then, one day after taking a series of tests, I learned something about myself. A teacher explained that the reason some things felt harder for me was because I had **dyslexia**.

Dyslexia means my brain reads and processes words a little differently than some other people. It didn't mean I was dumb. It just meant my mind worked in its own unique way. At first, I didn't know how to feel, but the more I learned about **dyslexia**, the more I became aware of myself and why I learned the way I did.

Some people think dyslexia means you have trouble reading only. However, dyslexia can affect people in different ways. Some people have trouble reading words, while others have trouble with numbers, directions, or remembering steps.

Reading wasn't the hardest thing for me; math was. It was challenging to understand numbers, rounding, and some math steps. My brain saw symbols and patterns differently.

I now knew that I too could learn.

With a little extra help, I could understand.

I could explain what I learned.

I was permitted to stop calling myself the dumb one.

Permitted to learn differently.

Permitted to like reading more than math.

Permitted to be creative.

Permitted to think in color.

Permitted to be me!

PERMITTED

I wasn't broken.

I wasn't slow.

I just learned differently.

I wasn't the dumb one!

I was the imaginative one.

The storyteller.

The word speller.

The girl who could turn confusion into clever sentences, dizziness into creative paragraphs, and captivating stories.

One day, my words will rise, and they will speak for me. I will be the writer, the speaker, the author. And everyone will finally see what I've come to learn and love about myself.

I am Different, Not Dumb!

CREATIVE

Different, NOT Dumb deals with **self-perception**, **dyslexia**, and **learning differences**. These questions can guide students to think about:

- words and labels
- feelings
- learning styles
- empathy
- confidence

Understanding the Story

1. Do you think the word "dumb" is a kind or hurtful word? Why?
2. Why did the main character start to believe she was dumb?
3. How do you think the main character felt when she didn't understand the lessons in class?
4. What did the main character learn about herself later in the story?

Thinking About Learning

5. What does it mean to learn differently?
6. Do you think everyone learns the same way? Why or why not?
7. What is something that is easy for you to learn?
8. What is something that is harder for you to learn?

Empathy and Kindness

9. How can we help someone who is struggling to understand something in class?
10. Why is it important to be kind when someone is learning something new?

Personal Reflection

11. Have you ever felt like the main character?

Connecting to the Message

12. What do you think the author wants readers to learn from this story?

ABOUT THE AUTHOR

J. Postell is an author, publisher, speaker, and writing advocate with more than 15 years of experience working with students from elementary through high school. She attended Southern New Hampshire University, where she studied Creative Writing and English with a concentration in Fiction.

Her passion for writing began in childhood. In fact, her mother often joked that she wrote on everything she could find—including the walls. At eight years old, J. was diagnosed with dyslexia, a challenge that shaped her educational journey but never defined her potential. Instead, it deepened her commitment to helping young people understand that learning differences do not determine intelligence or success.

J. Postell has authored several books and has helped publish numerous others through her work in independent publishing. She is also the creator of **Junior Authors**, a youth writing initiative designed to introduce young writers to the publishing process and encourage creativity and confidence through storytelling.

Through her writing and educational work, J. Postell continues to encourage young people, especially those who learn differently, to embrace their creativity, believe in their voice, and recognize that being different does not mean being less capable.

www.ingramcontent.com/pod-product-compliance
Lightning Source LLC
LaVergne TN
LVHW052301100826
845147LV00001B/111